Things to Know Before Starting or Investing in a Electricity trading company

First published by Kjøller 2023

Table of Contents

Introduction

Electricity trading is a complex and rapidly evolving field, where the slightest misstep can lead to disastrous consequences. Before engaging in such a venture, it is important to understand the intricacies of the industry and the associated jargon. This book, "Things to Know Before Starting or Investing in an Electricity Trading Company," serves as a valuable resource for both novices and seasoned professionals. The glossary format provides clear and concise definitions for the essential terminologies in electricity trading. With this book, readers can navigate this volatile industry with confidence and make informed decisions that align with their business objectives.

Ancillary services

Additional services that support the grid's stability and reliability, such as frequency regulation, voltage control, and reactive power support. They are necessary to maintain the balance between electricity generation and consumption within a power system. Electricity trading companies often specialize in providing ancillary services, making it a profitable source of revenue for them.

Arbitrage

The practice of taking advantage of price differences in various markets to make risk-free profits. Electricity traders can engage in arbitrage by buying electricity at a lower price in one market and then selling it in a higher-priced market. Efficient arbitrage requires deep knowledge of market trends, price mechanisms, and trading strategies.

Asset management

The supervision and maintenance of an electrical trading company's physical assets, including power plants, transmission lines, and distribution systems. Asset management involves the acquisition, operation, and optimal utilization of assets to ensure financial stability and maximize profits. By investing in efficient asset management practices, traders can mitigate operational and financial risks.

Auction

A competitive bidding process where electricity traders can buy or sell electricity at an agreed-upon price. Auctions can be either forward or spot, allowing traders to either buy or sell electricity for delivery during a future period or at the current moment. Auctions are commonly held by grid operators, power exchanges, and traders to maximize profits and manage risks.

Backhaul

Backhaul refers to the movement of electricity from areas of excess supply to areas of high demand. This is often done to avoid congestion on the power grid and prevent blackouts.

Balancing Authority (BA)

A BA is responsible for maintaining the balance between the supply and demand of electricity within a specific geographic region or control area. They are tasked with making real-time adjustments to the power grid to ensure there is enough electricity to meet current demand.

Balancing Coordinator

The balancing coordinator is responsible for coordinating the supply and demand of electricity within a specific geographic region or control area. They have the authority to make real-time adjustments to the power grid to ensure reliability and stability.

Balancing Energy

Balancing energy is the additional electricity that is needed to balance the supply and demand of electricity in real-time. Balancing energy is often provided by generators that are capable of ramping up or down quickly to meet changing demand.

Balancing Market

The balancing market is where electricity traders can buy and sell balancing energy. The market is used to balance the supply and demand of electricity in real-time.

Baseload

This is the minimum amount of electricity demand that exists on the power grid at any given time. Baseload power is typically provided by large, efficient power plants that operate continuously.

Bid

A bid is an offer to buy or sell a certain amount of electricity at a specified price. Bids are typically submitted to the wholesale electricity market and are used to determine the market clearing price.

Bilateral Contract

This is an agreement between two parties in which they agree to buy and sell a certain amount of electricity at a specified price. Bilateral contracts are often used by electricity traders to hedge against price fluctuations in the wholesale electricity market.

Blackout

A blackout is a complete loss of power to a large area or region. Blackouts can be caused by a variety of factors, including equipment failure, severe weather, or lack of generation capacity.

Broker

A broker is an intermediary between buyers and sellers in the electricity market. They connect buyers and sellers and facilitate the buying and selling of electricity.

Capacity Auction

An auction in which electricity providers bid to supply a certain amount of electricity over a specified time period. Capacity auctions are commonly used in capacity market systems to ensure adequate electricity supplies and grid reliability.

Capacity Factor

The ratio of the actual output of a power plant to its maximum output over a given time period. Capacity factor is an important metric for electricity trading companies because it affects the profitability of power plants and the responsiveness of supply to demand.

Capacity Market

An electricity market structure in which electricity providers are paid to maintain the ability to generate electricity in the future. Capacity markets are designed to ensure power reliability and cost-effectiveness by incentivizing generators to invest in new capacity and keep existing plants open.

Carbon Market

A market designed to reduce greenhouse gas emissions by creating a financial incentive to reduce emissions. Carbon markets can provide trading opportunities for electricity trading companies that generate low-carbon electricity or have offset projects. They can also be subject to regulatory and political uncertainties, which can introduce risks.

Centralized Market

An electricity market structure in which electricity is traded on a centralized platform. Centralized markets can be more efficient than decentralized markets because they enable price discovery, reduce transaction costs, and improve liquidity.

Clearinghouse

A central entity that matches buyers and sellers in electricity markets. Clearinghouses enable participants to buy and sell power with confidence, knowing that the settlement process is efficient and reliable. They also provide transparency and facilitate price discovery.

Congestion

Occurs when the demand for electricity exceeds the available transmission capacity to deliver it to consumers. Congestion can lead to price spikes, power outages, and other problems. Electricity trading companies must stay on top of congestion patterns and develop strategies to mitigate the impacts.

Contingency Reserve

A reserve of electricity generation or transmission capacity that is held in reserve to address unexpected events such as equipment failures, extreme weather, or unforeseen surges in demand. Contingency reserves are essential for maintaining power system reliability.

Counterparty Risk

The risk that one of the parties in an electricity transaction will default on their obligation to deliver or pay for electricity. Counterparty risk can be managed with tools such as collateral requirements, credit screening, and hedging strategies.

Curtailment

The deliberate reduction in electricity generation or consumption in response to market or grid conditions. Curtailment is often used to balance the supply and demand of electricity in real-time and maintain system stability. Electricity trading companies must be able to predict and respond to curtailment events to maximize profits.

Electricity Load Forecasting

Load forecasting is the process of predicting the amount of electricity that will be needed to meet the demand of consumers. Accurate load forecasting helps electricity trading companies buy and sell electricity at the right time, improving their profits. Load forecasting uses machine learning algorithms, statistical techniques, and weather data to predict future electricity consumption.

Electricity Market

A platform where buyers and sellers trade electricity as a commodity. It is regulated by a market operator or an independent system operator (ISO) that ensures the reliability and fairness of the market. Investors in electricity trading companies should understand the structure of the electricity market, including the types of participants, types of contracts, and market rules to make informed decisions.

Electricity Market Design

Electricity market design refers to the rules, mechanisms, and incentives that govern electricity markets. It includes pricing mechanisms, demand response programs, and renewable portfolio standards, among others. Electricity trading companies should be aware of the market design in their operating region and understand how it affects their trading strategies and profitability.

Electricity Trading Strategies

There are many trading strategies that electricity trading companies can use to maximize their profits. The most common ones include day-ahead trading, real-time trading, and capacity trading. Day-ahead trading involves buying and selling electricity for the following day, while real-time trading is done on the day of delivery. Capacity trading involves reserving transmission capacity and selling the rights to use it.

Electricity Transmission Network

A network of high voltage power lines that transport electricity from power plants to distribution substations. Understanding the transmission network's capacity and congestion is essential for electricity trading companies as it affects pricing dynamics and trading strategies.

Energy Contracting

Energy contracts are legally binding agreements between energy buyers and sellers. Electricity trading companies must understand the different types of contracts, including power purchase agreements (PPAs), tolling agreements, and capacity contracts, among others. They should be able to negotiate favorable terms and conditions to manage their risks effectively.

Energy Market Regulation

Electricity trading companies must comply with various regulations governing energy markets to avoid legal issues and penalties. Regulatory bodies impose rules and standards for market participants and ensure fairness and transparency in the market.

Energy Risk Management

Energy risk management involves identifying and mitigating risks associated with energy trading, including market risk, credit risk, operational risk, and compliance risk. Electricity trading companies should have a robust risk management strategy in place to avoid losses and ensure business continuity.

Energy Storage

Energy storage systems allow electricity trading companies to store and discharge energy on demand. It enables them to buy electricity when prices are low and sell when prices are high, making them more competitive in the market. Energy storage can also provide ancillary services like frequency regulation and spinning reserves, which add revenue streams to electricity trading companies.

Energy Trading Software

Advanced software tools are critical for electricity trading companies to analyze the market, make trading decisions, and optimize their operations. Energy trading software automates processes, provides real-time market analysis, and enables electricity trading companies to manage their risk effectively.

Financial Transmission Rights (FTR)

A financial instrument that allows electricity traders to hedge financial risks associated with congestion on transmission lines. FTR traders essentially buy the right to receive or pay compensation if the price difference between two points along the transmission line exceeds a predetermined level. This helps ensure that they can recover potential losses associated with power trading.

Firm Power

Electricity generated by a power plant or energy source that is available on demand, regardless of weather, equipment failures, or other unforeseen circumstances. It is often used to meet peak power demand or for emergency backup power. Electricity trading companies can buy and sell firm power in the market, and profits can be significant, especially during high-demand periods.

Fixed Costs

The expenses that an electricity producer must bear regardless of how much energy is generated, including operating costs, maintenance, and financing. Fixed costs can be significant and are paid by consumers through their electricity bills. Trading firms need to factor in fixed costs when making trading decisions to ensure sufficient profitability.

Flexibility

The ability of an electricity trading company to respond to changing market conditions with agility and efficiency. Flexibility is essential for traders to optimize trading strategies and maximize profits. This can be achieved by having diverse portfolios, adaptive trading systems, and effective risk management practices.

Fluctuations

Sudden and unpredictable changes in electricity supply, demand or price. Fluctuations are a common occurrence in the electricity market, driven by changing market conditions, weather, or other factors. Trading firms need to be able to manage risks associated with fluctuations, for example by hedging with forward contracts, FTRs or other financial instruments.

Forecasting

The process of predicting future developments in electricity supply and demand. Forecasting is essential for electricity trading firms to plan ahead and make informed trading decisions. Accurate forecasting can help trading firms to determine the timing, volume, and pricing of their trades to maximize profit. Forecasting can also help grid operators to balance supply and demand, minimize costs and avoid blackouts or disruptions.

Forward Contract

A legally binding agreement that allows electricity traders to buy or sell energy at a predetermined price for a specific date or period in the future. Trading firms can use such contracts to secure prices and manage risks associated with fluctuations in energy prices. The contract obligates the buyer to purchase energy at the agreed price, and the seller to sell energy at the same price, regardless of market conditions. It is not the same as a Futures Contract, which is standardized and traded on exchanges.

Frequency Regulation

A service provided by the system operator to maintain stable frequency and keep the grid balanced. The frequency can be impacted by changes in demand, supply, or unexpected outages. To maintain balance, the system operator can adjust power output or absorb power from generators very quickly. Electricity trading firms can provide frequency regulation services to the grid in exchange for payments.

Fuel Mix

The combination of energy sources used to generate electricity. It can include coal, natural gas, nuclear, and renewables such as wind, solar, and hydro. Electricity trading firms need to be aware of the fuel mix to make informed trading decisions based on supply, demand, and market conditions.

Fuel Price Risk

The financial risks associated with changes in fuel prices. Electricity trading firms need to be aware of fuel price risk, which can impact the profitability of their trades. They can use financial instruments such as forward contracts, swaps, or options to hedge against any unexpected price fluctuations.

Gas Turbine

A type of engine that uses natural gas to generate electricity. Gas turbines are used in power plants to provide baseload power or peak-load power when demand is high. Electricity trading companies must understand the gas turbine's efficiency, cost, and capacity to trade electricity profitably.

Generation

The process of producing electricity from a power plant. Electricity generation is the first step in the electricity supply chain, and electricity trading companies must monitor the electricity produced and its cost to trade fairly in the electricity market.

Generation Capacity

The maximum electrical power output that can be produced by a generator or a power plant. Electricity trading companies must understand the generation capacity of their suppliers to manage the electricity supply chain effectively, forecast electricity prices, and trade profitably.

Generator

The engine or turbine that converts mechanical energy into electrical energy. A generator is used in power plants to produce electricity that can be transmitted to customers. Electricity trading companies must understand the generator's capacity, output, and efficiency to trade electricity profitably.

Green Energy

Energy produced from renewable sources, such as wind, solar, hydroelectric, and geothermal. Electricity trading companies may focus on trading green energy to promote sustainability and reduce carbon footprint. They must understand the Green Energy requirements and compliance standards to trade green energy effectively.

Grid

The interconnected system of electric power transmission lines and substations that deliver electricity from power plants to customers. Electricity trading companies must understand the grid's capacity, transmission capabilities, and restrictions to manage their load balancing and ensure the smooth delivery of electricity.

Grid Balancing

The process of matching electricity demand with supply to maintain grid stability. Electricity trading companies must monitor the grid balancing mechanism to adjust the electricity price and ensure that the demand and supply are balanced, avoiding power outages or grid failures.

Grid Code

A set of technical and operational requirements that must be adhered to by anyone who connects to or uses the electricity grid. Electricity trading companies must comply with the Grid Code to ensure safe, reliable and efficient operation of the grid and to avoid penalties or fines.

Gross Pool

A term used in electricity markets to describe the total amount of electricity traded by all participants, including generators, retailers, and wholesalers. Electricity trading companies regularly monitor the gross pool to analyze the electricity market trends and forecast future prices.

Guaranteed Standards

The performance targets set by the electricity regulator that licensed suppliers must meet. These standards include the number and duration of power supply interruptions and response times to customer complaints. Electricity trading companies must ensure that their suppliers meet the Guaranteed Standards to maintain customer satisfaction and trust in the electricity supply chain.

Harmonic distortion

A term that refers to the excess vibration or electrical noise present in an electrical circuit due to the presence of non-linear loads. Non-linear loads, such as computers, variable speed drives, or other electronic equipment, cause harmonic distortion that can affect the quality of power supplied to the grid. Harmonic distortion can cause damage to equipment, increase energy consumption, and result in financial losses for electricity traders.

Heat rate

A measure of the efficiency of a power plant in generating electricity. Heat rate represents the amount of energy in British thermal units (BTUs) required to produce one kilowatt-hour (kWh) of electricity. Lower heat rates indicate that a plant is more efficient in converting fuel to electricity, resulting in lower operating costs and higher profits for electricity traders. Heat rate is an essential metric for traders as it allows them to compare the performance of different power plants and assess their economic viability.

Hedging

A risk management strategy used by electricity traders to minimize or eliminate the potential impact of price fluctuations in energy markets. Hedging involves taking positions in financial instruments like futures or options contracts to offset potential losses in the physical electricity trading market. The goal of hedging is to protect the trader from adverse price movements while allowing them to benefit from favorable price movements. In electricity trading, hedging is crucial as energy prices can be very volatile, and traders must constantly manage their risk exposure.

High voltage transmission lines

Electrical power transmission lines that operate at voltages of 230 kV or above. High voltage transmission lines are used to transport electricity over long distances, typically from power plants to distribution networks. They are designed to minimize power losses and ensure a reliable supply of electricity to consumers. Electricity traders must consider the impact of high voltage transmission lines on the energy market and their potential risks and opportunities.

Hourly pricing

A pricing structure where the price of electricity changes every hour based on the supply and demand dynamics in the market. Hourly pricing is prevalent in electricity markets that use real-time pricing systems. Traders must carefully analyze market trends to forecast the hourly prices and make profitable trades. Hourly pricing can be highly volatile, and traders must have access to real-time data and effective risk management strategies to succeed in this market.

Hydroelectric power

A renewable energy source that generates electricity by harnessing the energy of falling or moving water. Hydroelectric power plants use turbines to convert the kinetic energy of water into electrical energy. Hydroelectric power is a reliable and clean energy source that can help meet the growing demand for electricity while reducing greenhouse gas emissions. In electricity trading, traders may invest in hydroelectric power companies or participate in hydroelectric power purchase agreements.

Hydrogen fuel cells

A clean energy technology that generates electricity by combining hydrogen and oxygen in an electrochemical process. Hydrogen fuel cells are a promising option for powering homes, vehicles, and other applications that require electricity. Electricity traders may invest in companies that produce hydrogen fuel cells or participate in hydrogen fuel cell development projects.

Imbalance

Imbalance is a term used to describe the difference between the predicted energy production or consumption and the actual amount of energy produced or consumed. It's a common challenge for electricity trading companies as it can result in penalties, reduced profits, and other financial losses. To mitigate the risk of imbalance, companies must have accurate forecasting tools, effective hedging strategies, and a deep understanding of the market dynamics.

Incentive-based regulation

Incentive-based regulation is a regulatory approach used in the electricity industry to encourage companies to invest in improving their infrastructure, reducing operational costs, and providing more reliable service to customers. Regulatory bodies such as the Federal Energy Regulatory Commission (FERC) and state utility commissions use incentive-based regulation to motivate electricity trading companies to make investments that benefit their customers while maximizing profits. Understanding the impact of incentive-based regulation on their operations is vital for investors looking to invest in electricity trading companies.

Independent System Operator (ISO)

An ISO is an organization responsible for managing and controlling the transmission of electricity across a particular energy market. The ISO is responsible for ensuring that supply and demand are balanced, and that the grid remains stable and reliable at all times. Investors in electricity trading companies should understand the role of the ISO in the market where they operate, as it can have a significant impact on the company's operations and profitability.

Information Technology (IT) systems

Electricity trading companies rely heavily on IT systems to monitor and manage their energy portfolios. Advanced IT systems are necessary to improve forecasting accuracy, optimize trading strategies, and manage risk effectively. Investing in robust IT infrastructure and data analytics tools can provide a competitive edge in the market, allowing for more efficient and profitable trading operations.

Interactive Energy Trading (IET)

IET is an automated trading system that allows electricity trading companies to buy and sell energy in real-time. It provides traders with access to the latest market data, pricing, and other critical information needed to make informed trading decisions. IET systems are essential for operating in today's fast-paced, complex energy markets, and are increasingly being adopted by electricity trading companies worldwide.

Interconnection

Interconnection is a term used to describe the linking of power grids, allowing for the transfer of electricity between two or more systems. This can be beneficial for a company that operates in an area with limited energy resources or is looking to diversify its sources of power. Interconnection agreements must be negotiated among the parties involved and approved by regulatory bodies to ensure reliability, safety, and fair compensation for all parties involved.

Intra-day trading

Intra-day trading refers to the buying and selling of electricity on the same day of delivery. It's a high-risk, high-reward trading strategy that requires a deep understanding of supply and demand dynamics, market trends, and the impact of weather and other external factors. Investors in electricity trading companies should be aware of the potential rewards and risks associated with intra-day trading and understand how their portfolio is impacted by this type of trading activity.

Investment Grade

Investment Grade is a credit rating assigned to a company or investment based on its level of creditworthiness. For electricity trading companies, an investment-grade rating is critical to gaining access to capital markets, securing financing, and attracting investors. Rating agencies such as Moody's and Standard & Poor's assess a company's financial performance, growth prospects, and other factors before issuing an investment-grade rating.

Investor-owned Utilities (IOU)

IOUs are publicly traded companies that provide electricity, natural gas, or water to customers in a regulated market. These companies are heavily regulated by state and federal agencies and are required to provide affordable and reliable service to their customers. For investors looking to invest in the electricity market, IOUs can provide a stable source of revenue with relatively low risk, compared to other market players such as independent power producers.

J-curve effect

The j-curve effect refers to a temporary increase in costs or losses before a new investment or initiative generates significant benefits or profits. Electricity trading companies may face j-curve effects when they invest in new technologies, infrastructure, or markets. The j-curve effect can be managed by careful planning, risk assessment, and strategic investment decisions that balance short-term costs with long-term gains.

JEPX

JEPX is the Japan Electric Power Exchange, a marketplace for trading electricity in Japan. JEPX provides transparent, competitive, and efficient trading services to electricity suppliers and customers, helping to promote cost-efficiency and stability in the electricity market. JEPX also supports the integration of renewable energy by facilitating the trading of renewable energy credits and promoting the use of clean energy sources.

JERA

JERA is a Japanese energy company that specializes in electricity generation, trading, and fuel procurement. JERA is one of the largest electricity companies in Japan and is committed to promoting the transition to a sustainable energy future. JERA invests in renewable energy projects, supports energy efficiency measures, and works closely with communities to promote energy conservation and awareness.

Joint bidding

Joint bidding is a strategy in which multiple electricity trading companies collaborate to bid for electricity supply contracts or tenders. Joint bidding can help companies reduce costs, increase competitiveness, and share risk. Joint bidding requires effective communication, trust, and coordination among participating companies, as well as clear guidelines and agreements on issues such as pricing, distribution of profits, and decision-making.

Joint dispatch

Joint dispatch is a coordinated system in which multiple electricity generation and transmission companies work together to optimize electricity supply and demand. Joint dispatch can help reduce costs, improve efficiency, and promote renewable energy integration. Companies that participate in joint dispatch must have reliable and flexible infrastructure and be able to respond quickly to changing demand and supply conditions.

Joint venture

A joint venture is a business agreement between two or more parties to invest or operate in a specific project or sector, such as electricity trading. Joint ventures allow companies to pool resources, expertise, and technology to reduce costs, maximize profits, and expand their market share. Joint ventures can also provide a platform for companies to enter new markets or develop new products or services.

Jolt

A jolt refers to a sudden increase in electricity prices. It can be caused by various factors, such as an unexpected power outage or a surge in demand. Jolts can have significant impacts on electricity trading companies, as they must act quickly to secure electricity supply and mitigate losses. Companies can manage risks associated with jolts by developing effective risk management strategies and hedging techniques to protect themselves from sudden price spikes.

Jurisdiction

Jurisdiction refers to the legal authority of a government or regulatory body over an electricity trading company. Electricity trading is subject to various regulations, laws, and policies at national, state, and local levels, which can have significant impacts on company operations and profitability. Companies must understand the regulatory framework within which they operate and comply with relevant requirements to avoid penalties or legal disputes.

Just transition

Just transition refers to the principle of ensuring that the transition to a low-carbon economy is fair and equitable for all stakeholders, including workers, communities, and investors. Electricity trading companies can play an important role in promoting just transition by investing in renewable energy, supporting green jobs, and engaging with local communities. Companies must also ensure that their operations do not cause harm to the environment or contribute to climate change.

Kapacity (Capacity)

The maximum amount of electricity that a generator or transmission line can produce or carry. Capacity is typically measured in megawatts (MW) or gigawatts (GW) and is an important factor in electricity trading. Companies that sell electricity must ensure they have enough capacity to meet customer demand while also managing the costs associated with unused or excess capacity.

Karoo Basin

A region in South Africa that is rich in coal reserves and has become a major source of energy for the country. Electricity trading companies that operate in South Africa often rely on coal-fired power plants in the Karoo Basin to generate electricity, making it an important region for energy investors and traders.

Key Performance Indicators (KPIs)

Metrics that are used to evaluate the performance of a business or organization. In the context of electricity trading, KPIs might include factors such as the volume of electricity traded, the profitability of trades, and the reliability of the transmission and distribution networks. KPIs provide companies with a way to measure their success and identify areas for improvement.

Kilowatt-Hour (kWh)

A unit of energy measurement equal to the energy consumed by a 1,000-watt appliance in one hour. It is the standard unit of measurement for electricity consumption and billing. Electricity trading companies use kWh to track the amount of energy traded and calculate billing rates for customers.

Knot

A unit of measurement for the speed of a ship, equal to one nautical mile per hour. In electricity trading, the term "knot" is often used to refer to the speed at which electricity is transmitted through a power line. This can affect the efficiency and reliability of the transmission and is an important consideration for companies that trade in electricity.

KVA (Kilovolt-Ampere)

A unit of measurement for the apparent power of an electrical circuit. KVA is used to measure the maximum amount of power that can be delivered to a load, regardless of whether it is being used efficiently. This is an important consideration for electricity trading companies, as they need to ensure that they have enough KVA capacity to meet customer demand without overloading the transmission lines or causing other issues.

Kwacha

The currency of Zambia, which is a major producer and exporter of electricity in sub-Saharan Africa. Kwacha is often used to price electricity trades in this region, and fluctuations in the value of the currency can affect the profitability of these trades.

KYC (Know Your Customer)

The process of verifying the identity of a customer before entering into a business relationship with them. In electricity trading, KYC helps companies establish the credibility of their counterparties and reduce the risk of fraud or money laundering. This includes verifying the legal status, financial stability, and reputation of the counterparty. KYC is typically done before a trade is executed and helps ensure that both parties have confidence in the transaction.

Kyoto Protocol

An international agreement signed in 1997 to address the issue of climate change by setting targets for reducing greenhouse gas emissions. The Kyoto Protocol has had a significant impact on electricity trading, as companies are now required to factor in the cost of carbon emissions when calculating the cost of generating and selling electricity. This has led to the development of new trading strategies that take into account the environmental impact of electricity production.

Levelized Cost of Electricity (LCOE)

LCOE is a measure used by electricity trading companies to estimate the cost of producing electricity over its lifetime. LCOE takes into account the capital costs, operating costs, fuel costs, and any subsidies or incentives associated with production. LCOE helps electricity trading companies to compare different sources of energy and determine the most cost-effective way to produce electricity.

Line Losses

Line losses refer to the loss of electricity that occurs during transmission and distribution over power lines. Line losses are typically caused by resistance, heat, and electromagnetic interference. Electricity trading companies try to minimize line losses by using higher voltage lines, reducing the distance of transmission, and improving the efficiency of power transformers.

LMP (Locational Marginal Pricing)

LMP is a market-based pricing mechanism used by electricity trading companies to set the price of electricity at different locations in the grid. LMP takes into account the transmission costs, generation costs, and losses associated with delivering electricity from one location to another. LMP encourages electricity trading companies to build new generation facilities where they are most needed, and it incentivizes consumers to reduce their electricity consumption during peak periods.

Load Curtailment

Load curtailment is the practice of reducing or shutting down power consumption when there is an excess demand for electricity or an insufficient supply of electricity. Load curtailment can be voluntary or involuntary, and it is typically done through demand response programs or emergency measures. Load curtailment helps to maintain grid stability, prevent blackouts, and reduce greenhouse gas emissions.

Load Following

Load following refers to the practice of adjusting the production of electricity to match the fluctuating demand in real-time. Electricity trading companies use various techniques such as grid monitoring, demand response, and energy storage systems to match the supply and demand of electricity. Load following is critical to maintaining grid stability, minimizing blackouts, and ensuring the reliability of the electricity supply.

Load Forecasting

This refers to the process of predicting the amount of electricity that will be required to meet the consumer demand in a particular area or region. Accurate load forecasting helps electricity trading companies to plan their operations, manage their resources, and avoid over-supply or under-supply situations. Load forecasting is influenced by factors such as weather, time of day, seasonal changes, and economic growth. Electricity trading companies use various techniques such as statistical analysis, machine learning, and artificial intelligence to forecast the electricity load accurately.

Load Growth

Load growth refers to the increase in electricity demand over time. Load growth can be influenced by factors such as population growth, economic development, weather conditions, and technological changes. Electricity trading companies use load growth projections to plan their operations, expand their infrastructure, and mitigate the risks associated with over-supply or under-supply of electricity.

Load Profile

A load profile is a graphical representation of the electricity consumption patterns of a particular consumer or group of consumers over time. Load profiles can help electricity trading companies to understand the electricity requirements of different consumers, segment their market, and develop customized pricing strategies. Load profiles are influenced by factors such as the type of industry, location, and seasonality.

Load Shedding

Load shedding is the deliberate controlled reduction of electricity supply to certain areas or consumers during periods of high demand or insufficient supply. Load shedding is typically used as a last resort measure to prevent grid-wide blackouts or damage to electrical infrastructure. Load shedding can be selective or rotating, and it is usually implemented through automatic or manual control systems. Load shedding can have economic and social impacts, and it is a controversial measure that requires careful planning and communication.

Long-term Contracts

Long-term contracts are agreements between electricity trading companies and consumers to supply or purchase electricity at a fixed price for an extended period. These contracts are beneficial to both parties as they provide certainty and stability in pricing, production, and consumption. Long-term contracts help electricity trading companies to secure financing, invest in infrastructure, and reduce price volatility risks. Consumers benefit from lower prices, guaranteed supplies, and steady production. Long-term contracts typically last for several years, and they can be tailored to meet the needs of both parties.

Marginal Cost

The Marginal Cost is the cost of producing an additional unit of electricity. It is calculated by dividing the change in total cost by the change in output. In power markets, the Marginal Cost is an important factor in determining the dispatch order of generators, as generators with lower Marginal Costs are typically dispatched first. When electricity demand is low, only the most efficient and lowest-cost generators are dispatched, while as demand for electricity increases, the less efficient (and higher-cost) generators are brought online to meet the increased demand.

Market Clearing Price

The Market Clearing Price (MCP) is the price at which electricity is sold in a wholesale electricity market. It is determined by the intersection of the supply and demand curves in the market, and represents the cost of producing the marginal unit of electricity needed to meet demand. The MCP is an important indicator for electricity trading companies, as it determines the revenue they will receive for their electricity output.

Market Maker

A Market Maker is a company or individual that provides liquidity in a market. In the context of an electricity trading company, a Market Maker may be responsible for buying and selling electricity contracts to ensure there are always active bids and offers available in the market. They may also be responsible for managing risk associated with these trades, and for ensuring that the market remains fair and efficient.

Market Operator

A Market Operator is a regulatory body that manages and oversees a power market or exchange. They are responsible for maintaining a fair marketplace, establishing rules for market participants, and ensuring that electricity is delivered reliably and efficiently. A Market Operator also has the authority to allocate electricity transmission and distribution network capacity, and to coordinate the dispatch of electricity generators. In essence, they are the gatekeepers of the power market, and play an essential role in ensuring that the market functions smoothly and efficiently.

Market Power

Market Power refers to the ability of a company or group of companies to influence the price or availability of a good or service in a market. In the context of an electricity trading company, market power can be a significant concern, as it can lead to higher prices and reduced competition. Market power may be abused through the use of anti-competitive behaviors like price-fixing, bundling, or exclusive dealing arrangements.

Merchant Plant

A Merchant Plant is a power generation facility that operates without any long-term power purchase agreements or other contracts. Instead, it relies on spot market prices or other market mechanisms to sell its electricity output. Merchant plants are typically owned and operated by independent power producers or merchant generators, and they may be subject to greater price volatility and risk than plants with long-term contracts.

Meter Data Management

Meter Data Management (MDM) refers to the process of collecting, validating, storing, and processing data from meters. MDM systems are used by electricity trading companies to manage and analyze data from multiple sources, and to ensure that customer billing is accurate and timely. They may also be used to identify inefficiencies or other opportunities to optimize grid operations and to monitor the performance of renewable energy assets.

Metering

Metering refers to the process of measuring and recording the usage of electricity. In the context of an electricity trading company, accurate metering is critical to ensuring that customers are billed correctly, and that the company's revenue streams are accurate. Metering technology has improved significantly in recent years, with the development of more sophisticated devices such as smart meters, which can provide detailed data on electricity usage in real-time.

Metering Point

A Metering Point is the location where electricity consumption is measured and recorded. It may be a physical meter on a customer's property or within a building, or it may be a virtual "point" in the electricity grid. Metering Points are important for tracking electricity usage and billing customers accurately. In some cases, Metering Points may also be used to measure and record electricity output from distributed generation facilities like rooftop solar panels or wind turbines.

Microgrid

A Microgrid is a localized electricity network that can operate independently of the main grid. It typically consists of a combination of generators, storage devices, and load management systems that can be controlled and operated by a single entity. Microgrids are becoming increasingly popular in areas where grid infrastructure is limited, unreliable or where there is a need for improved resilience against power outages or natural disasters. A Microgrid may also be used in combination with the main grid to provide backup power or help reduce overall demand during peak periods.

Off-Grid Solutions

It is a decentralized electricity generation system that operates independently of the main grid. Off-grid solutions can range from small-scale solar power systems, wind turbines, or micro-hydro facilities. These solutions are often adopted by businesses or communities located in remote areas where grid connectivity is limited or expensive, or in areas facing frequent interruptions in power supply.

Off-Peak Hour Trading

A trading strategy that involves buying electricity during times of low demand or off-peak hours and selling it during high demand or peak hours. Off-peak hours typically occur during the night and early morning when factories and businesses are closed. This trading strategy requires a good understanding of the electricity market and the fluctuation of prices through various times of the day, month, and season.

Open Access

It refers to the ability of multiple electricity generators and traders to access the power grid on a non-discriminatory basis. The concept of open access is essential for promoting competition, efficient pricing, and ensuring that the grid is used in the most optimal way possible.

Open Market

It is a market structure in which a large number of buyers and sellers interact in the buying and selling of goods or services, with the price determined through the forces of supply and demand. In the context of electricity trading, an open market structure is one in which any generator or trader can participate, and the price is determined through a competitive bidding process.

Operating Cost

It is the cost of running or maintaining an electricity generation plant, including fuel, labor, maintenance, and administrative expenses. Understanding these costs is crucial for electricity traders, as it determines the profitability of the plant, and influences the decision to invest in new production facilities.

Operating Reserve

It is the additional generation capacity contracted by the system operator to balance any unforeseen changes in demand and supply. Thus, it acts as a form of insurance, and the system operator is responsible for ensuring that this capacity is available.

Operational Risk

It is the risk of loss arising from inadequate or failed processes, systems, or human errors. For electricity trading companies, operational risks may arise from system breakdowns, intermittent power supply, or mismanagement of contractual obligations, potentially resulting in significant financial losses.

Option

It is a financial instrument that gives the buyer the right, but not the obligation, to buy or sell a specific asset, such as electricity futures or options, at a predetermined price on or before a certain date. Options provide flexibility to electricity traders, allowing them to minimize the risk of price fluctuations, while also providing a potential for profit.

Outage

It is the unplanned shutdown or failure of an electricity generation unit or a transmission network component. Outages can occur due to natural disasters, equipment failures, or human errors, potentially disrupting the supply of power, and causing financial losses for power producers, traders, and consumers.

Over-the-Counter (OTC) Trading

It is the process of trading electricity outside the centralized market, meaning that the buyer and the seller deal directly with each other instead of using an intermediary. The OTC market may provide flexibility and speed of transactions, but it may also result in a lack of transparency and exposure to credit risks.

Peak demand

The period of highest energy usage during a given day or season, often occurring in the late afternoon or early evening when people return home from work and turn on lights, appliances, and HVAC systems. Electricity trading companies must be able to predict and manage peak demand in order to ensure a reliable supply of electricity to customers.

Physical electricity trading

The buying and selling of actual physical electricity, rather than financial contracts or derivatives based on electricity prices. Physical electricity trading requires expertise in power systems engineering, risk management, and supply chain logistics.

Portfolio management

The process of actively managing a diversified portfolio of electricity assets, such as power plants, renewable energy projects, and financial contracts. Effective portfolio management requires careful analysis of market trends, risk assessment, and strategic decision-making.

Power exchange

An electronic marketplace where electricity trading companies can buy and sell electricity contracts, options, and futures. Power exchanges often have standardized contracts with fixed terms and pricing, providing a level of transparency and liquidity in the electricity trading market.

Power grid

An interconnected system of power generation, transmission, and distribution infrastructure that delivers electricity from power plants to consumers. Electricity trading companies must understand the structure and functioning of the power grid in order to buy and sell electricity effectively.

Power pool

An organized market where electricity generators can sell their output to buyers, and where electricity trading companies can buy and sell electricity at market prices. In some regions, power pools are operated by independent organizations that facilitate trading among multiple buyers and sellers.

Power Purchase Agreement (PPA)

A contract between an electricity generator and a buyer to purchase electricity at an agreed-upon price over a certain time period. PPAs often involve renewable energy sources, such as solar or wind power, and have become an important tool for promoting investment in renewable energy projects.

Power system reliability

The ability of an electricity system to deliver a consistent, reliable supply of electricity to customers at all times. Electricity trading companies must collaborate with other industry players, such as grid operators and utilities, to ensure that the power system remains stable and resilient in the face of changing demand, weather events, and other challenges.

Price volatility

The degree to which energy prices fluctuate over time, often influenced by factors such as weather, supply and demand, or geopolitical events. Electricity trading companies must stay informed about price trends and fluctuations in order to make profitable trades and manage risk effectively.

Public utility commissions (PUCs)

State or federal regulatory bodies that oversee the activities of electricity providers, including electricity trading companies. PUCs are responsible for ensuring fair pricing, reliable service, and environmental standards in the electricity industry.

Qualifying Facilities (QFs)

Refers to small-scale electricity generation facilities that meet specific criteria set by the Federal Energy Regulatory Commission (FERC). QFs are often renewable energy sources such as solar, wind, and hydropower, and they are eligible for special rates and tariffs. By incentivizing small-scale renewable energy production, the government promotes competition and diversification in the energy industry, leading to a more sustainable and efficient power system. QFs are increasingly popular among electricity trading companies, as they provide an opportunity to expand their energy portfolios and meet climate targets.

Quality Assurance (QA)

Refers to the processes and procedures used by an electricity trading company to ensure that the energy produced and sold meets industry standards. QA includes monitoring production processes, conducting tests, and verifying that the energy produced meets the required specifications. Quality assurance is an essential component of QoS, ensuring that customers receive the expected level of service and reliability from their electricity trading company.

Quality of Supply (QoS)

Refers to the level of power supply that an electricity trading company provides to its customers. This metric measures the reliability of power supply and the consistency of the voltage level. It is essential to maintain QoS as customers rely heavily on electricity and require a stable supply to operate their electrical devices. QoS is also crucial in ensuring the efficient operation of factories and businesses that require a continuous power supply. A good electricity trading company must prioritize maintaining high QoS standards to ensure customer satisfaction and attract more investors.

Quantity Risk

Refers to the risk associated with fluctuations in energy demand or supply. Quantity risk can significantly affect an electricity trading company's profitability, and companies must manage it effectively to remain competitive. Risk management strategies such as hedging, quota allocation, and diversification can help minimize quantity risk, ensuring that the company can produce energy at a consistent level and meet customer demand.

Quantum of Energy (QoE)

Refers to the amount of electrical energy that an electricity trading company produces, purchases, or sells. QoE is measured in kilowatt-hours (kWh) and is essential in determining the company's revenue and profitability. Energy traders use QoE as a tool to predict future demand trends and plan production schedules in advance. QoE also plays a crucial role in setting tariffs and pricing structures for different customer segments. High QoE is essential for an electricity trading company as it allows the company to capture a significant market share and outperform competitors.

Quarantine Power

Refers to the energy capacity held in reserve to handle sudden spikes in demand or unpredictable supply shortages. Quarantine power is essential for an electricity trading company to maintain QoS, ensuring that customers receive a reliable power supply at all times. In the event of a power outage or shortage, quarantine power can be quickly released to fill the gap, stabilizing the grid and preventing blackouts.

Quasi-Regulated Market

Refers to a market structure that is partially regulated by the government but operates with market-based principles. In a quasi-regulated market, the government sets policies and guidelines but leaves the pricing structure and production decisions to the free market. Electricity trading companies operating in quasi-regulated markets must navigate regulatory frameworks while considering market factors such as demand, supply, and pricing fluctuations.

Quick Response Power (QRP)

Refers to the ability to respond quickly to sudden changes in energy demand or supply. QRP is essential for an electricity trading company to ensure that the grid remains stable and balanced. By quickly adjusting production levels, companies can prevent blackouts or surges in the grid, which can cause significant damage to electrical devices. Investing in technology that enables quick response power can boost the efficiency and profitability of an electricity trading company.

Quorum

Refers to the minimum number of participants required to make a decision in a power trading market. Quorum is an essential element of governance in power trading, ensuring that decisions made by participants are legitimate and representative of the market's views. Quorum levels can vary depending on the size of the market, with larger markets requiring higher levels of quorum to prevent decision-making gridlock.

Quota Allocation

Refers to the process of allocating a fixed amount of energy to a particular customer or segment. Quota allocation is commonly used in the power trading industry to manage supply and demand imbalances. It allows electricity trading companies to distribute energy among their customers using a fair and transparent mechanism. Quota allocation can be used to incentivize customers to reduce their energy consumption during peak demand periods, leading to a more efficient use of resources.

Real-time pricing

The dynamic pricing system that reflects changes in electricity demand and supply. Electricity trading companies need to be aware of this pricing to hedge their energy purchases and to sell it forward to clients.

Regional Transmission Organizations (RTO)

RTO manages the bulk transmission of electricity in specific geographical regions. Trading companies must work closely with these organizations to identify opportunities to buy and sell electricity at the optimal price.

Regulatory compliance

Electricity trading companies must comply with various regulations and guidelines by statutory authorities. Compliance is crucial for the long-term sustainability of the business and avoiding legal penalties.

Renewable energy

Energy generated from natural and renewable sources such as sunlight, wind, and water, that can be used instead of non-renewable sources like coal, oil, and gas. Starting or investing in an electricity trading company requires a sound understanding of renewable energy sources and their pricing dynamics.

Renewable Energy Certificates (REC)

A tradable commodity representing one megawatt-hour of electricity generated from renewable sources. Companies can buy RECs to meet regulatory standards or offset carbon emissions. Trading companies must understand REC pricing and redemption rates to provide clients with competitive pricing options.

Renewable Energy Credits (REC)

REC is a tradable certificate representing proof that one megawatt-hour (MWh) of electricity was generated from a renewable energy resource. Investors can buy RECs to meet regulatory requirements and to keep their carbon footprint low.

Renewable Portfolio Standard (RPS)

A legislation mandating a certain portion of energy generation to be from renewable energy sources by a specific date. Understanding the RPS requirements of the states you operate in is critical for electricity trading firms to devise their business strategy.

Reserve margin

The amount of excess energy capacity that electricity grids maintain in reserve to handle unexpected imbalances in the demand and supply of electricity. Understanding reserve margins is key to developing a profitable trading strategy.

Resistance

A material's ability to oppose an electric current. Resistance is an important factor in determining the efficiency of transmission and distribution of electricity through a given network.

Retail electricity provider

A company that sells electricity directly to residential or commercial customers. Retail electricity providers must comply with regulations stipulated by the Public Utility Commission (PUC).

Scheduling

The process of determining the amount of energy that will be generated by a power plant and the time it will be delivered to the grid. Electricity trading companies need to have effective scheduling processes in place to ensure that they can meet the energy demands of their customers.

Settlement

The process of financial reconciliation between a generator and a consumer. Electricity trading companies need to ensure that there is a settlement process in place that accurately reflects the energy consumed and generated by the parties involved. Settlements are typically carried out on a daily, weekly, or monthly basis.

Smart grid

An electricity network that uses digital technology to monitor, control, and optimize the distribution of electricity. Electricity trading companies can benefit from a smart grid as it improves energy efficiency and reduces costs.

Tariffs

These are structured rates approved by the regulatory authorities that determine the cost of electricity for end-users. Electricity trading companies must be aware of the tariffs in their target market, as they affect the price at which they can buy and sell electricity.

Tradable certificates

Also known as Renewable Energy Certificates (RECs), these are credits that certify the production of a certain amount of renewable energy. RECs can be bought and sold on trading platforms, which provide an additional source of revenue for electricity traders and incentive for renewable energy production.

Trading margin

This is the difference between the price at which an electricity trader buys and sells energy products. It is the primary source of revenue for trading companies and must be monitored closely to ensure profitability.

Trading platform

This is an online portal where electricity traders buy and sell energy products. A reliable trading platform should provide transparency, security, and efficient trade processing. Before starting an electricity trading company, evaluate the available trading platforms in the market and select the one that best suits your needs.

Trading strategy

Electricity traders use various trading strategies to maximize their profit margins. These include hedging, arbitrage, and speculation. Traders must select a trading strategy that best suits the market conditions and their financial objectives.

Trading volume

This refers to the amount of energy products bought and sold by electricity traders. Trading volume affects the revenue, market share, and market influence of electricity trading companies.

Transmission congestion

When the electricity demand exceeds the available transmission capacity, transmission congestion occurs. Electricity traders need to be aware of congestion patterns in the transmission network to make informed trading decisions and avoid penalties.

Transmission line

These are high voltage cables that transmit electricity over long distances from the power plant to the distribution points. Before investing in an electricity trading company, it is crucial to understand the transmission network in the region to determine the costs of electricity delivery and potential income.

Transmission losses

These refer to the amount of electric energy lost as heat during transmission over long distances. Electricity traders need to factor in transmission losses in their pricing decisions to ensure profitability.

Transmission pricing

These are the charges levied by the transmission line operators to transport electricity from the power plant to the distribution points. Electricity traders need to understand the transmission pricing structure to estimate their costs and determine their profit margin.

Ultra-low emission zone (ULEZ)

A designated area in which vehicles must meet certain emission standards in order to enter. ULEZs are becoming more common in cities around the world, and may have an impact on the electricity industry through increased demand for electric vehicles and charging infrastructure. Investors should be aware of the potential opportunities and challenges associated with ULEZs.

Unbundling

The separation of different functions in the electricity industry, such as generation, transmission, and distribution. Unbundling allows for competition in the market and may lead to lower prices for consumers. However, investors should be aware of the potential risks associated with investing in unbundled companies, such as increased competition and regulatory challenges.

Unconventional energy sources

A term used to describe sources of energy that are not traditionally used in the electricity industry, such as geothermal, tidal, or biomass energy. Unconventional energy sources may offer potential opportunities for investors, but may also be subject to regulatory challenges and technological limitations. Investors should be aware of the potential benefits and risks associated with unconventional energy sources and the companies that produce or use them.

Under-frequency load shedding (UFLS)

A technique used by grid operators to maintain system stability during times of high demand or low supply. UFLS involves the intentional shedding of load

Unified Energy System (UES)

A term used to describe the electricity system in Russia, which was formerly a state-owned monopoly. The UES was unbundled and privatized in the early 2000s, and is now composed of several companies involved in generation, transmission, and distribution. Investors should be aware of the regulatory environment and the competitive landscape in the Russian electricity industry.

Uninterrupted power supply (UPS)

A backup power source that can provide electricity during power outages or other disruptions. UPS systems are commonly used in data centers, hospitals, and other critical facilities to ensure continued operation. Investors should be aware of the various types of UPS systems and their potential uses in the electricity industry.

Uplift

A term used to describe the additional costs or payments associated with balancing electricity supply and demand on the grid. Uplift may be incurred by generators or consumers, and can be affected by factors such as weather, market conditions, and system constraints. Investors should be aware of the potential impact of uplift costs on the profitability of companies in the electricity industry.

Upstream

The segment of the electricity industry that involves the production of electricity, including generation and transmission. Upstream companies may include power plants, renewable energy sources, and high voltage transmission lines. Investors should be aware of the various technologies and methods used in upstream electricity production, as well as the potential risks associated with the industry.

Utility

A term used to describe a company that provides electricity to end-users or consumers. These companies are regulated by various government bodies and often have a monopoly in their service area. Investors should be aware of the regulations and restrictions that may affect the profitability and growth potential of a utility company.

Utilization rate

A measure of the amount of time that an electricity generator is in use, expressed as a percentage of total available time. Utilization rates can have a significant impact on a company's profitability and may be affected by factors such as demand, competition, and regulatory requirements. Investors should be aware of the utilization rates of companies they are considering investing in, as well as the potential risks associated with low or declining rates.

Validation

The process of verifying the accuracy and completeness of data used in electricity trading. Validation includes checking the entry of data, completeness of data, and reconciliation with external sources. Validation serves as an important step in ensuring accurate and timely energy transactions, which can make or break the performance of an electricity trading company.

Value at Risk (VaR)

The estimated maximum loss that an electricity trading company is likely to incur on its portfolio of energy assets over a certain time horizon, with a given level of confidence. VaR is a standard measure used by market participants to monitor and report the risk profile of their energy portfolios. It allows traders and investors to set appropriate limits and controls on their trading activities and to respond effectively to unexpected market events.

Variable Renewable Energy (VRE)

Renewable energy sources that are subject to variability and intermittency, such as wind and solar power. VRE sources pose unique challenges for operators and investors in electricity markets, including forecasting of energy production, integration into the grid, and pricing of energy products. Electricity trading companies need to incorporate VRE into their portfolio strategies to manage market risks and capitalize on opportunities.

Vesting

The process of transferring ownership of electricity generation assets from one party to another, typically to meet regulatory or contractual obligations. Vesting is a critical step in the trading of renewable energy certificates (RECs), which represent the environmental attributes associated with renewable electricity production. Electricity trading companies need to understand the vesting requirements in various jurisdictions and markets to ensure compliance and maximize the value of their RECs.

Vintage Year

The year in which a renewable energy facility begins commercial operation, used to determine the eligibility of renewable energy certificates (RECs) for compliance purposes. Vintage years are critical in determining the value of RECs, as market demand for certain vintages can vary depending on regulatory compliance requirements and other factors. Electricity trading companies need to be able to track and forecast vintage year supply and demand dynamics to effectively manage their RECs portfolios.

Virtual Financial Transmission Rights (V-FTR)

A form of financial instrument used to hedge transmission congestion risks in electricity markets. V-FTRs allow buyers and sellers to allocate congestion costs in a transparent and efficient manner, enhancing the reliability and cost-effectiveness of energy trading. V-FTRs are an essential tool for electricity trading companies to manage transmission risk and optimize their portfolios.

Virtual Power Plants

An aggregation of decentralized energy resources that can be managed as a single entity in electricity markets. Virtual power plants (VPPs) allow electricity trading companies to optimize the use of renewable energy, storage systems, and other distributed energy resources to provide reliable capacity, balancing services, and other energy products. VPPs can also provide ancillary services, such as frequency regulation and voltage support, that are essential for maintaining grid stability and reliability.

Volatility

The degree of variation or unpredictability in energy prices, demand, or supply. Volatility is a key driver of risk and reward in energy trading, and can have a significant impact on the performance of an electricity trading company. Managing volatility requires accurate modeling of market dynamics, effective risk management strategies, and agility in responding to unexpected events. Electricity trading companies need to be able to measure and manage volatility across various energy products and regions to generate returns for investors and stakeholders.

Voltage Support

The provision of reactive power or other services aimed at maintaining appropriate voltage levels in electricity grids. Voltage support is critical for maintaining the stability and reliability of the grid, and is often provided by generators or other grid assets. Electricity trading companies need to be aware of voltage support requirements and constraints in various regions, as well as the impact of voltage support on energy prices and portfolio performance.

Volume Risk

The risk associated with trading a large volume of electricity at a fixed price. Electricity trading companies must be aware of volume risks, which can arise due to changes in demand, weather phenomena, or other unexpected factors. Managing volume risk requires a detailed understanding of market trends, regulatory changes, and future projections of energy demand, supply, and prices.

Watt

A watt is the unit of measurement used to quantify power or energy transfer rate, i.e. how quickly energy is used or generated. It represents one joule per second, which is the rate of energy transfer when work is done at the rate of one joule per second. A thorough understanding of the concept of watt is essential for electricity traders to develop trading strategies, manage energy supply and demand, and optimize pricing models based on energy consumption rates or generation capacity.

Weather derivatives

Weather derivatives are financial instruments used by electricity trading companies to manage risks associated with weather patterns, particularly in the energy sector. These derivatives are contracts with values that are determined by weather conditions such as temperature, rainfall, wind speeds, or other weather-related variables. They act as an insurance policy for companies that are vulnerable to weather-related risks and help reduce the impact of volatility in the energy market.

Weather patterns

Weather patterns play an integral role in electricity trading as they affect the demand and supply of energy. Understanding how weather conditions impact energy production, storage, and distribution can help electricity traders make informed decisions. For example, a heatwave or a cold spell can lead to an increase in energy demand for cooling or heating, leading to price spikes in the market. Seasonal variations in temperature also impact the demand for electricity, such as winter months leading to higher demand for heating homes or businesses. Thus, a thorough understanding of weather patterns is critical in electricity trading.

Wheeling

Wheeling refers to the transportation of electricity over transmission lines owned by a third party, from one location to another. It enables energy consumers to buy electricity from sources beyond their immediate service territory, increasing the market access to a wider range of power producers, and providing better pricing options. Electricity trading companies need to understand wheeling arrangements and how it impacts the cost of energy, transmission fees, and reliability of supply.

Wholesale electricity market rules

Wholesale electricity market rules refer to the regulations and policies of electricity trading operations established by ISOs, RTOs, and government agencies. These rules govern a wide range of market activities such as pricing mechanisms, market participants, transmission capacity, and delivery protocols. Electricity trading companies must be familiar with these market rules to comply with regulations, maximize profits, and minimize the risk of legal or financial penalties.

Wholesale electricity price

The wholesale electricity price refers to the cost of electricity as traded in the wholesale market. It is influenced by multiple factors such as market competition, fuel prices, demand, and supply dynamics, and renewable energy policies. Electricity trading companies need to keep track of the wholesale electricity price to optimize their trading strategies, profit margins, and risk management practices.

Wholesale energy market

The term "wholesale energy market" refers to the marketplace where energy producers and consumers trade in bulk amounts of electricity, gas or other forms of energy, typically on a regional or national scale. These markets are regulated by independent system operators (ISOs) and regional transmission organizations (RTOs) and often involve power generators, transmission owners, and grid operators. Understanding the fundamentals of the wholesale energy market is essential before starting or investing in an electricity trading company, as it determines the pricing and availability of energy supply, and influences the company's profitability.

Wholesale energy suppliers

Wholesale energy suppliers refer to companies that produce and sell energy in large quantities in the wholesale market. These suppliers can be power generating companies, natural gas producers, or renewable energy companies. Wholesale energy suppliers play a vital role in the energy market as they influence pricing, availability, and reliability of supply. Understanding the competitive landscape of wholesale energy suppliers is essential for electricity trading companies to optimize their trading strategies, pricing models, and supply chain management.

Wires charges

Wires charges refer to the costs for electric transmission and distribution services, such as the operation and maintenance of power lines and substations, incurred by electricity suppliers. In the United States, these charges are regulated by the Federal Energy Regulatory Commission (FERC) and are typically priced at a fixed rate per kilowatt-hour (kWh). Understanding wires charges is crucial for electricity traders to develop cost-effective trading strategies, pricing models and manage financial risk.

Workforce training

Workforce training refers to initiatives for training employees of an electricity trading company. It is essential to have a well-trained workforce to effectively manage the complexities of energy trading operations. Training programs must focus on risk management, trading strategies, technical analysis, renewable energy policies, and regulatory compliance, among other topics. Continuous training and skill development programs can improve the company's overall performance, reduce the risk of errors, and increase employee retention.

www.ingramcontent.com/pod-product-compliance
Lightning Source LLC
Chambersburg PA
CBHW071027220526
45467CB00004B/1542